Finally

Understanding Money

What you should have been taught

*Your Simple Money Rules for
reaching financial freedom on almost ANY income!*

Based on the

15/85 Money Law

First Edition

by B. P. Van Cleve

**Published by RockLedger, Inc.
Vero Beach, Florida**

Dedicated to Robert S. Van Cleve
The author's grandfather, who inspired this work.

Copyright 2020

Preface

The idea for this book came from a conversation I had about 9 years ago with an older businessman who was quite successful in his life and was trying to help a young man who worked for him to make good personal financial decisions. He was frustrated because this young guy had never learned basic sound financial lessons and had no basis for making good choices. He suggested I should conduct public classes as part of my Accounting business, open to the public. The idea was people would pay a small amount to learn what they had never been taught at home or in school.

I never got around to putting on classes, but instead I started compiling notes on personal finances. This book is the organization of those notes.

An author should have a good reason to write a book on a topic. Either they feel their message is not being adequately written about or feels what is being said is wrong or too complex. I see a lot of pronouncements like, "These are the 5 things you must do to…" with no explanation behind the recommendation as to why they make the recommendation. I like to know the "why" of something in order for me to be persuaded.

I find many self-help books typically contain one good idea that the author builds an entire book around, and therefore ends up repeating themselves over and over, making slight variations on how they say the same thing, all to fill up a certain thickness of book. I find this really irritating, and usually don't end up reading the entire book.

In this book I hope to teach basic rules about winning when it comes to money. This book covers not just abstract theory but how to actually implement them. I deal with the "big picture" of finances, the *why* to do these things, so that you get a good understanding.

This book is not about making a static budget, which I think is a waste of time. I won't talk about how to clip grocery coupons to save. I won't teach you how to be a penny-pinching miser.

This book is for anyone, young or old, who wants to do things better when it comes to money, who wants to learn sound principles of managing the spending of their income to gain the most out of it, whatever the income's size.

These principles should be taught in schools and by parents to prepare their children for life. Sadly, many enter adulthood woefully unprepared to handle money, and spend a lifetime making poor choices, and have little to show for years of hard work. Others seem to do well on modest incomes. What's the difference? **Knowledge, attitudes, and habits.**

You won't find any secrets here, no magic formulas (except for one), mostly just a common sense approach. No get-rich-quick schemes or how to earn lots of money for little work. I've included do-it-yourself worksheets, instructions, everything you'll need to wrestle control of what money passes through your hands in order to win at money.

What I hope to accomplish in your thinking is that in order to solve any financial difficulties, you must first understand the situation you're in and the problems you have. This book is intended to help you frame the problems and the goals, and when you do, your solutions will present themselves. Sometimes, all it takes is someone like me to say something in a certain way to make everything clear. That's what I hope to accomplish. To clarify, to simplify your goals with money.

Contents

Acknowledgements

I thank the following people for help with this book:
Victor and Sheryl Raley.

Introduction

How we deal with money is one of the most important aspects of our lives. Right up there with who we marry, where we live, what we do for a living, or who we are friends with.

Your lifestyle must be based on <u>your</u> <u>income</u>, not the apparent lifestyle of someone else you're trying to keep up with or impress. Do they pay your bills? No. So, what other people think of you is really none of your business.

Balance is crucial. Spending yourself into extreme debt does not lead to anything but misery. Being a tightwad is not living either. Both extremes lead to miserable existences. Happiness is achieved by attaining <u>balance</u>.

You've got a life to live. It can't be just work and paying bills and trying to save for the future. You have to make room for vacation, entertainment, sports, recreation, travel, reading, movies, concerts. Balance your life. Find lots of time for re-charging your batteries- you'll be happier, and have more energy.

The following is a list of some of the bigger ideas I will cover in this book:

What is the real goal of how you handle money?

Van Cleve Rule Number One: Your income never…

Van Cleve Rule Number Two: Save… and Spend…

Doing things in order. Prioritizing. Deciding what is important.

First solvency, then security, then success. (In that order.)

First establishment, then accumulation, then retirement.

The concept of reserves.

The concepts around insurances.

The concepts about credit.

Living a simpler life.

Essential and discretionary spending.

SECTION ONE

SOLVENCY

Chapter 1

Long Term Objectives

Why manage?

The reason we want to manage our money is for the individual or the family unit to obtain the maximum **happiness** from our current spending while at the same time maintaining *solvency*, building *security*, and striving for *independence*.

What defines happiness? Answer:
A mind free from fear and worry.

What do you mean by independence? Answer:
Independence means you can **meet all your obligations** without taking on debt you cannot easily repay.

Happiness and Independence are accomplished through setting Long-Term Objectives and Prioritizing.

It has nothing to do with a high or a low income- it's how you **spend** what you make that counts.

I'm not saying you have to be debt-free. It would be nice but not always realistic. I recently read that the average used car price was now over $20,000. You need a car, in most cases, before you've managed to save up that much money.

The first thing I recommend is to think about and write down your own long-term objectives. Realize that money is nothing more than a tool. It is worthless by itself. Worthless? Yes. Coins are just cheap metal and the rest is just nice paper. It's what you plan to use it for that is important to achieving your personal long-term goals.

Example of the goals to achieve by way of your Long Term Objectives in General:

- To be more independent financially.
- To not spend every dime you make.
- To not take on excessive, crippling debt.
- To live a more balanced life.
- To avoid extremes.
- To live a simpler life.
- To not be thrown into a tizzy when an emergency pops up.
- To understand human nature as it relates to money.
- To get better at prioritizing.
- To get better at planning.
- To do things in their proper order.
- To stop trying to take short-cuts with money.
- To accept that it's normal to want a better life for yourself and your family.

Children are dependent. No grown up person wants to be **dependent**. Not just dependent on other person(s), but dependent on unfulfilling work just to make money to pay bills, or to have large debts to pay off with future earnings, which can be compared to having to carry around **heavy baggage**. To be avoided also are obligations because you felt you had to live up to a certain level of lifestyle. The more independence we can achieve- generally the happier, more relaxed, less stressed out we are.

Happiness is also attained when we have balance, and fewer extremes, in our lives. Extremes cause stress, and stress can make you sick physically. Sometimes we talk ourselves into the need to complicate our lives in order to advance. The human mind is a problem-solving machine that sometimes invents problems to solve. It is not true that life has to be more complicated, most of the time it's *simplifying* our lives that makes us more productive, and certainly more happy.

Wouldn't it be nice when an emergency pops up and not having to stress out over the money needed to fix it, because you have **reserves** you can tap. And realize right now that this is possible on any income. You have *told* yourself that it's not possible because you spend everything you make. It's really that simple. Here's a hint about the magic rule I'll talk about later- *adjust your lifestyle to 85% of whatever you make.*

Understand and accept this basic law of human behavior: Our human brains are problem-solving machines. We can always figure out a way to spend the money that comes into our hands. Resist this mental reflex. It is counter-productive to your long-term financial health.

Learning to manage anything is largely **developing the ability to prioritize**, putting things (or to do things) in their proper order. Assigning relative importance is fundamental to your financial planning to achieve your own personal priorities. It defeats the above-mentioned mental reflex.

I advocate doing things in order. That is why I say become **solvent** comes first. Don't seek shortcuts. Seeking **success** before you've achieved **solvency** is a long shot. Have people taken big risks and won the lottery? Sure, but do you ever hear about the 98% or the millions who lose? Of course not. You never hear about the losers.

Some people try to gain power over you by slowing you down. They try to make you feel guilty for wanting more. It is not wrong to want a better life for yourself and your family. You are the only one responsible for your life. No-one else. Avoid controlling people.

Capitalism is not a dirty word. Capitalism merely refers to free-market competition which creates better products for lower prices and the free-flow of money to where it's best used. It's actually when freedom is interfered with that injustices arise. Our competitive, striving system generally brings others along with us. Capitalism is a system that frees people to cooperate with others more fully to achieve things. It's the opposite of people controlling other people.

Only short-cutters and law breakers bring harm to others when they advance because they're doing so at someone else's expense. It is completely normal for you to want a better life.

Do you have a purpose in your life? It seems like some have the attitude, "I didn't ask to be born, and so I'm going to just consume." We are not here to be mere consumers. On the following page are exercises, such as writing your own obituary. What did you do with your life? List everything you wish you had done. *Not satisfied with the result of what you've written*? You have a chance to get busy to change it. Eventually you may hit on something that stirs up **strong emotion**, and when you do…that's it! Our lives are short and precious.

Finally, I've included exercises for writing down your goals-lifetime, long-term, short-term goals, and daily habits or tasks. Work on these so that they make sense, shorter term things should lead to the longer term things and visa-versa; the longer term things should be supported by shorter term things that assist them. In other words, you don't want a long-term goal with nothing that gets you there. And all short-term goals should fit in with something longer term.

Some of what you read here might sound as if I'm referring to the financial management of a business. In a way, the individual, the family unit, is like a business. A business is simply an entity with one or more people, each with defined duties and responsibilities, working toward a common goal. The family is an important economic unit within society, if not the most important. Some in the family are breadwinners, others are dependent on them until they are ready to join the world and earn their own income. Children can be taught to have responsibilities and contribute to the whole, and learn the wise use of the family's income. The goal of the family unit, or the single individual, is the same as it is in a business, to grow, to achieve, to ***bear fruit***, to make this one life count. **Something is to result from life. I believe it's a sin to waste your life.**

Big picture recap:

1.) The goal with money is to achieve _______________
_____________ with whatever you earn.

Wrong answers include:
Accumulate a big pile of money for retirement and to leave for
your kids.
Buy the nicest stuff you can.
Impress your friends and family.
Be the envy of anyone else.

2.) You should first achieve ___________, then _____________, and
then _________________.

3.) Your _______________ never exceeds _____ _________ __
_________ __.

YOUR NOTES:

Stages of Life:	Approx. Age:	Focus should be:
Getting Established	20-35	Building the emergency fund Staying solvent Getting insurance
Accumulation	35-65	Build & use reserves Save toward retirement
Retirement	65 and over	Achieve the option to stop working for active income

Lifetime Goals:

Long Term Goals:

Short Term Goals:

Daily Tasks and Habits:

Obituary

Your Name Here
D.O.B - D.O.D

Summarize your life here.

My daily To-Do System:

Today's Top 3 Priorities

List the top, most important tasks to be done that day, things that advance one of your goals, not just routine tasks like brushing your teeth! (important, not urgent) Only work on these three, no others. If you don't get them all done, list those un-finished for the next day. It is important to only work off this list, and if you get side-tracked and distracted, get back to the list as soon as you're able. Make your list either first thing in the morning or the night before, whichever works better for you.

Chapter 2

Earning

In this book you won't learn how to make a big salary. You'll have to figure that out for yourself. No get-rich-quick schemes here either.

The various ways for you to make money:

- **Earned**- wages from working actively at a job or career.
- **Interest**- lending your money to someone or to a bank/institution.
- **Rental**- renting out an asset you own, like real estate.
- **Capital Gain**- increase value of an asset- can be realized or unrealized.
- **Dividend**- from owning a stock that pays one.
- **Profit**- from owning a business or selling something for more than you paid.

It's a good idea to have income from as many of these at the same time as you are able. It adds to your financial securityto not have *all your eggs in one basket.*

Ambition to earn money varies greatly among people and has nothing to do with brains. I've known some really dumb people who earned a lot of money and really intelligent people who just got by. People assign intelligence to ability to earn income but I've found in my lifetime no correlation. It's the drive, the ambition and the perseverance of the individual that differs.

Wanting to earn more is its own justification. Never feel like you have to explain yourself to others. Wanting more is good, it is natural, and it is healthy. It doesn't make you a bad person, or greedy. As long as you go about it ethically, are law-abiding, and aren't harming or neglecting others- go for it- you will be adding to life- yours and others around you.

One of the great things about our American system is that it is classless. What economic class you were born into does not dictate where you'll end up. *You do*. We are very class-mobile. The people on various lists you hear about year after year are not always the same people. We move in and out of classes. We have opportunity here. Here you have the freedom to move into a different class than you were born to… if you want. Are there obstacles which hinder you? Yes, of course. But we all have something that hinders our paths. What our American capitalistic systems strives for is to guarantee equality of opportunity. It does not guarantee equal outcome.

Maybe I'm an idealist but I think you should find work you love doing and then figure out how to get paid doing that. If all you work for is the money?… you do a bad piece of work. It's not the work result you're after… it's the coin. What would you think about a doctor who all they cared about was their fee? Our finest work is precisely that for which no-one could pay us. This explains why someone who seeks merely to duplicate another's work goes nowhere. One puts their soul into their work- the other just works for the money they'll make. One creates a work of art, demonstrating love, another, a sterile result. **Mercenary labor yields no fruit.**

Not everyone should be pushed to go to college. Likewise, they shouldn't be pushed to end up working for someone else. I was miserable for years as an employee.

A good exercise is to think back to your childhood. What types of activities did you lose yourself in doing, where time passed un-noticed, which energized you? Take the time to think about this, talk to others who remember you back then, and write all this down.

One of the most important things young people can do is aptitude and personality testing to discover their talents and tendencies, like the Myers Briggs, or StrengthFinder.

I believe we each have something at which we're gifted. Each of us has a special talent, a genius. Dan Sullivan, the business coach and author, calls this **Unique Ability**. I believe it is our duty to discover what this is. I think that when we discover our genius, that one thing we do so well and easily (that we don't even realize it because it comes so naturally for us) that we should find ways to spend the rest of our lives doing that. Take lots of tests. Discover all about you. It's not pointless navel-gazing. The quicker in life you find it, the happier you will be and the longer you'll have to share your talent with the rest of us.

The size of your income is not as important as what you do with the income you have. This is one of the main concepts I hope you get from this book.

This brings me to **Van Cleve Rule #1- Your income never exceeds your ability to spend it.**

Knowing this law of human nature requires us to adopt a rule for winning with money. It dictates the solution. ***Forget the notion that simply earning more will solve all your problems. It isn't true.***

Childhood Activities: Things you would naturally do and think about, that you could lose yourself in play for hours…

Tests to take:
Myers- Briggs __
StrengthFinder __
Keirsey __
DISC __
16 Personalities __

Your Unique Ability: (After reading Dan Sullivan's book)

A Visual Representation of the Ideas in this Book

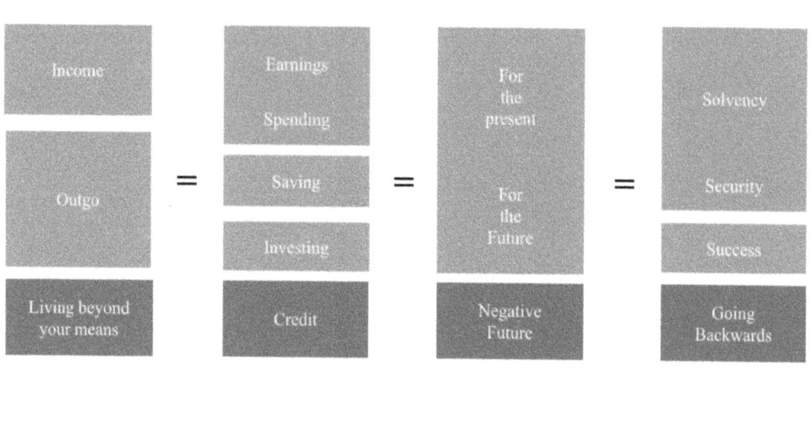

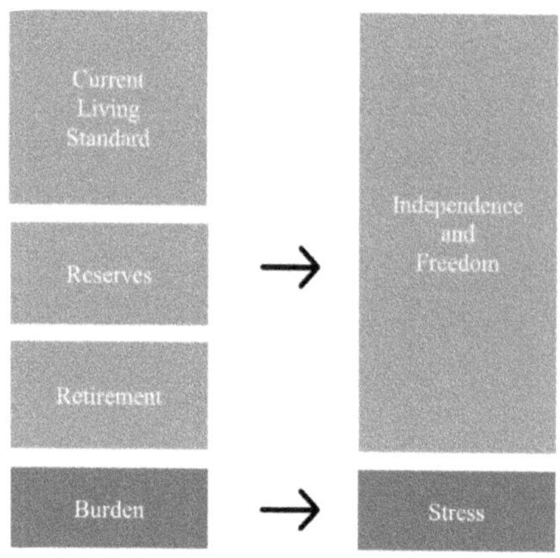

Chapter 3

Spending

As stated in **Van Cleve Rule #1, Your income never exceeds your ability to spend it.** The reason this is true is your mind, being a goal-seeking machine, will invent ways to spend. It will always come up with something you "need", something you have to have.

When you spend your income and try to save what's left over, there's usually little or nothing left, and saving seldom or never happens.

Given this, **Van Cleve Rule #2** states: **Save 15% of all income, no matter the source.** Make it a **rule**, not a plan. Why? Plans sometimes don't get done, rules happen every time. We'll talk later in another chapter what to save the 15% in.

The reciprocal of this is you start living on the **85%** of what your income is. Everyone can live on 85%, no matter the size of the income. You may need to ease into this. Or, at the least, do it through attrition- as you get increases in income, devote 100% of those increases to your 15% portion. When you have achieved this spending ratio, you're just going to **"pretend"** that 85% is all you have. And once you reach this ratio overall, when you get a bonus amount, or an increase, you can freely spend 85% of that!

It is a common misconception that if you only had a certain amount *more* of income, that would fix things. What ever that income level is that you think will solve all your problems, go ask someone who's already at that level, chances are they'll say they too "need" more income to be able to save. *The fact is we always seem to need more.* The trouble comes when we try to live a nicer lifestyle by **shortcuts** such as excessive credit (future) spending, which only makes the present less safe and less enjoyable.

OK, so you have 85% to work with. The next step in the process is to **prioritize** .the spending. Of the 85%, you break it into two broad categories; **essential** and **discretionary**.

Essentials are:

- Food
- Shelter
- Utilities
- Healthcare
- Transportation
- Insurance

Notes on essentials:

- **Food** is groceries, not eating out at restaurants.
- **Shelter** is rent or mortgage, property taxes, repairs, but not remodeling.
- **Cell phones** do not go into utilities unless your home does not have a landline, then count one main cell phone.
- **Healthcare** is health insurance, doctors, dentists, prescriptions.
- **Transportation** is the vehicle, gas, repairs needed for the vehicle to get to work only.

Pay essentials first, **always**. You will sleep well at night knowing the essentials are paid. Obviously you want to save money on these if you need to but they *always* get paid, and paid *before* anything else. **This is the essence of solvency**.

Everything else is discretionary. Including consumer debt repayment.

Discretionary spending is where the real cutting needs to come from. You don't "need" these things, oh you may "want" them, yes, but you won't really be **physically harmed** by not having them.

If you've already established a lifestyle that is out of line with this new model, this may mean you have to seriously adjust the essential portion, like your house, so you can afford more of the discretionary things you want from life. This will cause you to think long and hard about your priorities but the good news is you will be solidly meeting your situation like an adult… *Look at you! All growed up and adulting!*

Live simply, it's a better way. This doesn't mean you have to wear tattered rags and live in a shack, or never have any fun. Living simply means assigning things to their proper places, assigning priorities, and not living your life according to what you want others to think about you. The dirty little secret is that they aren't anyway, they are not thinking about you, they are only thinking about themselves.

Material possessions don't make you happy in the long run. People love you, things don't, so don't love possessions. Living well means living with integrity, being true to yourself, achieving love, finding truth, having liberty in your daily life. Nothing to do with possessions. Where life gets stressful and complicated is when we allow un-important things to take over.

At the end of the chapter is a model for a spreadsheet you can put together as a **dynamic budget**. It is dynamic (as opposed to a *static budget*)* in that you estimate future numbers but then replace with actual numbers as they happen. In a dynamic budget, you begin with all estimates based on past history AND what you think you can do with the numbers moving forward. Then as each month finishes, you replace the estimates for that month with the actual numbers and adjust future months (if you need to) better reflect reality. You end up with the most accurate assessment of how your year is going to turn out, and it alerts you as to whether you are meeting your goals.

* A static budget is what is done most often. Numbers are put down on paper and do not change throughout the year. I don't think static budgets are useful at all and I don't recommend doing them.

Doing a dynamic budget is entirely optional. It is more important that you simply live on the 85% of your total gross income.

At first, the 15% / 85% rule may seem obvious and overly simplistic and you may react by dismissing it because of that simplicity. Don't. It works precisely <u>because</u> it is simple. Using a specific number, 15%, imposes discipline. It defines the goal quantitatively, as opposed to just having a plan to "save more, someday" (Which never happens). Knowing something is one thing- doing it is quite another. Again, make it a rule, not a plan.

A sample dynamic budget:

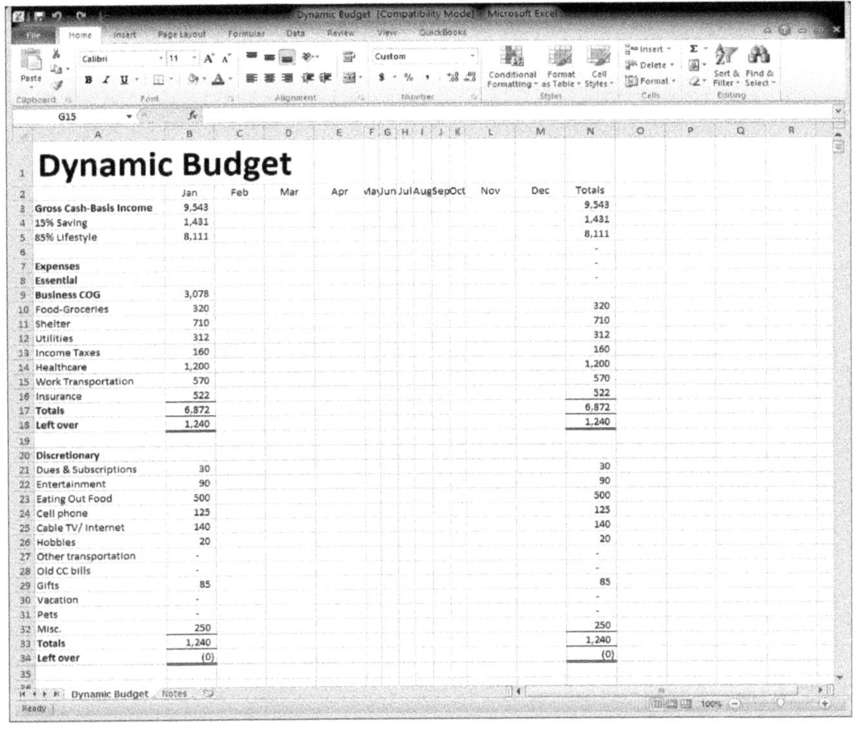

Dynamic Budget

	Jan	Feb	Mar	Apr	May	Jun	Jul	Aug	Sep	Oct	Nov	Dec	Totals
Gross Cash-Basis Income	9,543												9,543
15% Saving	1,431												1,431
85% Lifestyle	8,111												8,111
													-
Expenses													-
Essential													-
Business COG	3,078												
Food-Groceries	320												320
Shelter	710												710
Utilities	312												312
Income Taxes	160												160
Healthcare	1,200												1,200
Work Transportation	570												570
Insurance	522												522
Totals	6,872												6,872
Left over	1,240												1,240
Discretionary													
Dues & Subscriptions	30												30
Entertainment	90												90
Eating Out Food	500												500
Cell phone	125												125
Cable TV/ Internet	140												140
Hobbies	20												20
Other transportation	-												-
Old CC bills	-												-
Gifts	85												85
Vacation	-												-
Pets	-												-
Misc.	250												250
Totals	1,240												1,240
Left over	(0)												(0)

SECTION TWO

SECURITY

Chapter 4

SAVING

You are probably sick of hearing financial advisor types harp that we don't save enough. I know I am. They usually recommend saving between 10 and 20 percent of your income as best as you are able. What we actually save is not that much. We Americans have had years where we saved 1.9% and as much as 17%. From 1950-2000, we averaged 9.8%.

I propose that you make a commitment to an un-changing, steady, personal cardinal rule to save 15% of all income. If you make it a **rule** and not a suggested **goal**, you will more likely stick to it. You've made other rules you live by; like always using your seat belt while driving, turning off your cell phone during dinner or at the movie theater, or always putting your car keys by the door.

This method is available to everyone right now, right where you are, and the good news is you don't need anyone's help, you can do this all by yourself. You have everything you need right now, right where you are to achieve your own financial stability. You don't need to hire a financial or life coach, you've got this.

As I've stated already, you might need to ease into this plan if your lifestyle currently consumes all your income. You might have to eliminate certain discretionary spending, put 100% of any increases in income or bonuses to savings until you can reach the 85-15 ratio. If this is the case, you should set a deadline to get this done within the next year. That's plenty of time to make the changes needed.

The secret to eliminating all your money troubles is deceptively simple. Just don't spend everything that you make. This advise might seem so obvious that you tend to dismiss it but that would be a mistake. Anyone, on any income, can practice this method. It doesn't matter how much you make if you live on just 85% of your income, that's all there is to it. You "pretend" that is all you have to work with. I understand this may be very difficult to do at first, but making this a cardinal rule to live by will change your life. I am a strong believer in keeping things simple, and part of making things simple is instituting new rules to live by.

What income do you apply this rule to? ***All income, no matter what the source.*** Any time you make a deposit or cash someone's check, get cash from someone, 85% is yours to spend as you wish. Again, keep it simple by making no exceptions. Handling money doesn't need to be complicated or stressful.

No exceptions, done each time, immediately upon receiving. That part is important. Do not put this off to later. A rule… not a plan. Never postpone or skipped. Treat it like a must-do act.

Notes:

All income, the gross amount of paychecks, from whatever the source, even cash gifts.

401(k) deductions or any savings type deduction from paychecks counts toward the 15% you're saving, but not the company match, only your portion. It's easy if you can do an online transfer to your savings, which can be at you bank, done online or done online at an outside bank like Ally.

Van Cleve Rule #2 states to save 15% of all gross income, no matter the source, and you'll never have to worry about money.

In the big picture, your financial life can be summed up as divided into three phases:
* getting **established** (age 20-35)
* **accumulation** of assets (age 35-65)
* and **retirement** (65 and beyond).

The primary goals you are after are:
* First **solvency**
* Then **security**
* Then **success**

In that order. And if you never get to the success, that's OK, don't sweat it, not everybody will. But you MUST start out solvent and always remain solvent. Then you add as much security to your base of solvency as you are able. Success is just the "icing on the cake". If you can create success, great, if not, you will have the satisfaction that you managed your finances well anyways.

In the **establishmen**t phase, the emphasis is on first creating and building an emergency fund and obtain insurances. The suggested amounts of the emergency fund range from $1,000 to 6 month's worth of expenses. I will leave it up to you what this figure should be but that's the range it should fall into. You should keep 1 month's expenses in your checking account as a cushion, which won't earn any interest but that's OK. The rest should be in a FDIC insured, interest bearing savings account, accessible within a couple days. Either your local bank or better yet an online account, like Ally, which pays a lot more interest. I'll talk in the next chapter about insurances. Again, the main goal in the establishment phase is solvency. Building a solid base.

In the **accumulation** phase, the emphasis is on building your lifetime assets. You'll want to increase your emergency fund to accommodate a larger lifestyle, and having good insurance coverage.

Building assets should include building **reserves** rather than relying on credit. Reserves are nothing more than anticipating future needs and saving for them. It is exactly the opposite of credit. This is also referred to as the *sinking fund* method. You would build reserves for things like replacing a car, furniture, new appliances, home remodeling, house down payment. These are big items that you can't buy insurance to cover. You can create a reserves chart like the one at the end of this chapter. You list the item needed, how much, when it's needed, then you prioritize the list. You would not have a reserve for damage to your house or car, except for the deductible, because those are insurable. But a new roof? Yes.

After doing this exercise, you may see that you can't possibly do it all. That's exactly the point. Now you need to prioritize and eliminate the lower priority items. See how this works? You are forcing yourself to live within 85% of your means.

But don't get discouraged and give up! Do not beat yourself up when you find out you can't have enough reserves. Just get busy whittling down your "needs". Maybe you can squeeze 2 more years out of that car, or the refrigerator will last longer than you think.

But I hear the objection, "that's what credit is for!" I would ask, if you can afford the credit monthly payment, which *includes interest* you are going to pay, you can afford to put away that amount to save up. And instead of paying interest, you are earning it. The difference is in when you get the thing, right?, now or later. That's why you start *before* you need the thing so that by the time

you need it, you have the money. Credit use should be limited to
something you absolutely need now but have not had enough time
to save up for. There should be few things that fit this criteria.

After solvency, the emphasis is security. After your emergency
fund and your reserves, then you can save money in (success)
longer term assets like stocks, bonds, mutual funds, real estate,
children's education. More on this in the Investing chapter.

When you start investing, find a good investment advisor. A good
one will help you be safe, diversified, balanced, I would
recommend one who only charges commission when they actually
buy something, not as a percentage each year of what you have in
your portfolio, yet does not trade often or churn your account.

In the **retirement** phase, the emphasis is to be less dependent on
active, working income. The point is to have the ***option*** to work or
not. Some people want to keep working. Count me among them. I
have no interest in just sitting around or playing golf. How boring!
Actually the concept of not working at all in retirement is a fairly
recent one. It used to be people didn't live as long or they worked
until they physically could not any longer. The goal is for working
to be hopefully a *voluntary* option.

I do not agree with the notion of living poor so you can die rich
and leave your heirs a pile of cash. Believe it or not, you will not
be helping them. All that will do is make them lazy and feeling
entitled. It's perfectly fine to leave them a little legacy to get them
started in life with a little more help. Don't leave kids with a
fortune.

I get really tired of hearing that you need X dollars to retire. Few
are able to do that and all it does is discourage you. It de-motivates
you and causes you to stress out and think of yourself as a failure if
you're not able to meet that. Tune out all that poisonous thought
and just do your best.

The following is a reserves chart you could make:

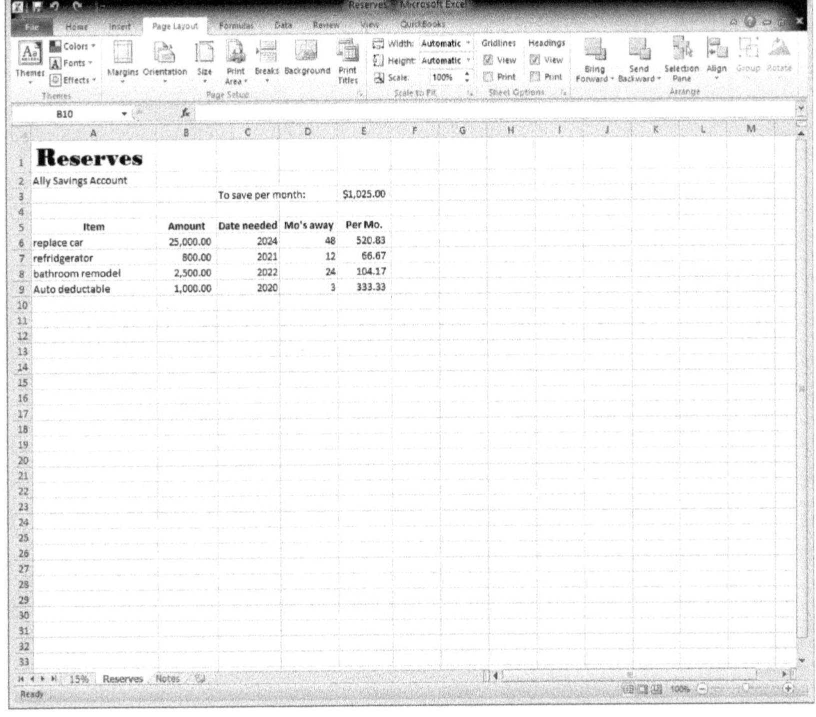

Chapter 5

INSURANCE

There are some bad attitudes out there about insurance that it is just wasted money. It's not. It may seem that way when you're just paying and paying but you have to understand what you're getting. You are getting protection from the risk of large losses. Insurance doesn't prevent accidents, fires, and illness; it does protect you from bearing the loss alone. By managing **risk**, insurance adds to your **solvency** and your **security**.

What is the function of insurance? To pool risk together with a lot of people to spread the risk to any one person against loss. Not everyone will have a loss yet the odds are someone will. So everyone pays a small amount to cover whoever the few are who will have a loss.

Types of insurance you should have:

- Auto
- Health
- Disability
- Home or Renter's
- Term Life
- Umbrella Liability

Auto- Only insure things that pose a real risk to you and avoid a bunch of add-ons. You don't need collision coverage on an old, junky car. You can raise the deductible to $500 or $1,000 to save money.

Term Life insurance- the best reason to have this is to cover the loss of future income of a breadwinner. A stay-at-home spouse should be covered because the surviving spouse would need to be able to hire a housekeeper and/or child care. There's no reason to have life insurance on children- you're not protecting income, forget protecting their "insurability" as they always pitch. Their insurance will still be cheap when they start buying it in their twenties and thirties. As you build up retirement assets, the need for life insurance theoretically goes away, especially where there's no more future working income to protect. Don't buy whole life that has savings attached to it- you can do much better saving on your own separately.

Disability insurance- a really good idea to have in place in case of a breadwinner not able to work. Aflac is an example.

Umbrella Liability insurance- it's very inexpensive insurance. It's cheap to add an "umbrella" policy of liability that takes over above and beyond your **auto** and **homeowners** limits are. People are very litigious today, some sue at the drop of a hat.

Find a good **insurance agent**- I like **Independent agents** who represent a number of companies so they can pick and choose the best for you. A good agent should be one that goes over your coverages every year or two. If your agent just takes your premium payments and renewals year after year and never consults with you, it's time to find a new one.

When or where *don't* you need insurance? Where or when no risk exists or you have plenty of funds to cover a relatively small loss. ***Don't buy extended warranties.*** They are in essence insurance policies. These companies have calculated the odds and are guaranteed to win, to make more money than they pay out. And you'll find they don't cover most likely things that go wrong anyway. You are better off saving yourself the money you would spend on the extended warranty, which would cover the odds of loss you may face.

Also, don't buy the following insurances:
- Heart attack
- Cancer
- Stroke
- Credit card payment protection
- Mortgage insurance (just cover with your regular term life)
- Accidental death
- Identity theft

Additional ways to save money:
- Bundle home and auto policies with the same company
- Keep your credit score good
- Pay premiums less frequently- semi-annual or annually

Chapter 6

CREDIT

Credit should only be used to buy an asset that does not depreciate in value, **a long-lived asset**, when the payment is <u>not</u> too burdensome on the monthly budget.

Notice how short this chapter is? That's a hint.

If the asset appreciates in value, like a house in a good neighborhood, or generates income, like business equipment , it's definitely OK to do.

And credit can be used if it's something really <u>needed</u> and there hasn't been time to save up for it in **reserves** described previously. So, it should not be used routinely or as the first choice.

Where credit is a bad choice is to buy anything that just gets **consumed** (not a long-lived asset). Things like general living expenses, vacations. Also things that **depreciate** in value make a lousy use of credit; cars, boats, motorcycles, RVs, furniture, mobile homes. And you don't necessarily need a brand-new car. Buy one that is a couple years old that the last guy took the depreciation hit on.

It can be a good idea to use a credit card for everyday and online purchases IF you are disciplined enough to resist impulse buying and you pay off the entire balance every month at least a week before the due date. Credit cards offer better fraud protection than debit cards, especially for online purchases. And, as Dave Ramsey has said, we tend to spend 15% more when using a credit cardso be careful. Creditors take their sweet-old time crediting your payment and then charge you the interest and a late fee, so always pay early.

That's all you need to know about credit unless you've overextended in it already and need to dig out of debt. This happens a lot because it's so easy to do. Lenders and credit card companies will gladly help you get deep in debt to them. They love it. ***Now they own you***. You work for them now.

Debt reduction is the one exception to the rule I've talked about when it comes to living in balance and not by extremes. To dig out of a debt hole, you're going to need to cut your spending in extreme ways and apply as much as you can to paying down the debt.

Do most people use credit to artificially raise their lifestyle? Sure, of course. But don't be like most people! When you owe someone money, they control you. You lose independence.

People have studied the attitudes and habits of self-made highly financially successful people. They all share the avoidance of using credit to enhance their lifestyle. They also avoid any form of gambling. *They* own their possessions, not the bank. Don't let others control you. ***Row your own boat.***

SECTION THREE

SUCCESS

Chapter 7

INVESTING

After saving exclusively to build your **emergency fund**, then next after you've started saving toward your **reserves** in a liquid savings account as described earlier, then above and beyond this you can begin **investing** for the longer term. The following are basic guidelines to get started on the right path. You are, and remain, solvent, you've built security, now you can work on the success.

Your investments should consist of:
- Stock Mutual Funds (financial) for growth
- Bond Mutual Funds (financial)for safety and balance
- Real Estate (home held personally and income property held inside an LLC)

Your financial investment "vehicles" (what the investment is inside of):
- Your 401(k) at work (if you have one)
- Roth IRA
- Traditional IRA
- Personal brokerage account
- An LLC to hold mortgaged (leveraged) rental property

General guiding principles to adopt:

- Max out your 401(k) to get the most **matching** amount by the company. The match is like free money that gives you an instant rate of return.

- Once 401(k) is maxed, then invest in Roth and traditional IRA's.

- If desired, income real estate (mortgaged) held in an LLC.

- Start as young as you can, the more **time** you have working for you, the better. Time is more important to building wealth than the actual dollars invested.

- Buy and hold. Do not attempt to trade frequently. Fees will eat up your money and you can't do as well or better than the pro's or the computers. Same goes for individual stocks.

- Buy low (or no) fee mutual funds. (Under 1.0%) The higher fee funds don't perform any better than the low fee or Index funds.

- Don't worry about **timing** the market other than in a very general, broad way. It's a better time to buy stock funds when everyone else is very pessimistic and visa versa. If you must try to time, be a contrarian to whatever the general mood of the market is.

- Be more in all **growth** when you're young, gradually add more conservative stocks and bonds as you get older, as you're getting closer to retirement from active work and are going to depend on retirement investments, you'll want safe investments mostly, because now time to recover from a downturn is less.

- Periodically (1-2 years) **re-balance** your portfolio. This means selling off enough of winners and buying other investments to maintain your desired ratio of stocks to bonds.

- Diversify between U.S. funds and International, stocks and bonds, financial and "hard" assets like gold. A good investment advisor will help you with all this.

- A good investment advisor? One who just charges a commission when they buy and sell, but doesn't "churn" your account with excessive activity. The other type charges a percentage of your portfolio each year. Don't use that type.

- Long term historically it is better to be in an **Index Fund**, they are lower cost and have beaten actively-invested funds, especially over longer time periods. The longer the time, the better a simple index fund does.

- Find an investment advisor who will meet with you at least annually. You will go over how your portfolio has done, determine any changes that need to be made, determine any re-balancing that's needed, and re-assess your goals and plans for the future.

Chapter 8

REAL ESTATE

I think real estate is one of the best investments you can make. Here are my reasons:

- You can control the investment, unlike stocks and bonds which "the market" makes go up and down totally out of your control.
- No taxes to pay every year on its appreciation (increase in value).
- It's tangible, real, you can see it and touch it. You can take pride in ownership.
- It's local.
- It is insurable against loss from damage.
- You have enforceable legal protection of leases for the income.
- Generates cash month after month. You make money while you *drool on your pillow*!
- You can leverage the ownership with low interest, long term loans. Try that with stocks and bonds. Very risky!
- You can delegate any work or management you don't want to do.
- It's passive income. You're not trading hours and freedom for dollars like in a job.
- You can even postpone capital gains when you sell doing a 1031 like-kind exchange.
- Very low overhead to operate. No expensive storefront or office needed.
- You can put each property inside an LLC to protect your other, personal assets.

I think real estate is superior to other investments such as stocks, bonds, and mutual funds for these reasons. With them you are completely at the mercy of the market, no control, dividend cash generation is very small, you can't postpone capital gains, on mutual funds you pay taxes every year whether you take the money or not, they're hard and risky to leverage or to protect from loss. *About the only downside to real estate is it's not liquid.*

- Home- often your biggest asset and your biggest liability.
- Raw Land- no income and zoning determines everything you will be allowed to do.
- Residential Rentals- easiest to acquire but requires the most management.
- Commercial/Industrial rentals- less management than residential.

Your home is likely the biggest single one of your investments you'll ever make. Choosing right is therefore really important to your finances. Here are some rules of thumb:

- The home price should be limited to 2 1/2 times the family annual income.
- Housing costs in total should be no more than 30% of your spending budget.
- A 20% down payment would be needed to avoid PMI. (private mortgage insurance)

It's better in general to buy the worst house on the block rather than the best house on the block. You'll get a better deal and you can then make improvements up to the standard of the other houses, without "over" improving for the neighborhood. Over improving makes it more difficult to get your money invested back out when you sell.

Buy into the best neighborhood you can afford. The value will hold and grow the better the neighborhood is. What makes a good neighborhood? Closeness to grocery stores, far-ness from industrial areas (noise and smells), good public schools is a huge factor. All these factors will allow price growth (appreciation).

People who become wealthy tend to buy older (< 1975) homes in long-established neighborhoods and stay a long time. They generally don't build brand new McMansions as you might think. They also take their time in buying and are willing to walk away. They don't pay the initial asking price (unless they happen upon a genuine bargain). In other words, they don't "fall in love" with a property. Many times they find bargains by seeking house sales as a result of divorce, estates, and foreclosures.

For rental properties, make sure the zoning is correct- there are a lot of illegal conversions out there. Check into overall zoning and current use compliance. Check for easements. Obviously current leases in place are important and whether tenants are current on their rents. Evaluate whether the rents are in line with the market.

For rental income properties, residential is easier to get into because there's more of it and it's pretty straightforward- even if the economy is not great, people always need a place to live. It can be more of a pain to manage because of all the consumer laws that apply. For instance, if a unit is over 10-20 units, a resident manager (employees) may be required (now you're doing payroll). Annual inspections might be required. Avoid condo ownership, they generally don't appreciate well and can be plagued by litigation issues brought on by other owners, you could be placing yourself in the middle of a mess. And you lose a lot of control when dealing with an H.O.A.

Commercial / Industrial/ business is easier to manage but that doesn't mean no management as some might suggest. Commercial/Industrial tenants can go bankrupt or just go out of business. One real estate investor I knew would begin going around and soliciting businesses to move to his in other properties if he got even a *hint* that a tenant was thinking of leaving. He also kept his rents reasonable. Another of his criteria was to own a street front-type commercial property on streets where the speed limit was 35 or under. He actively tried to help his tenants succeed at their businesses. He was always 100% fully occupied.

Own the properties yourself personally or inside an LLC you own. Do not have partners or be a limited partner in someone's LLC, or invest in a Real Estate Investment Trust or REIT. ***Row your own boat***. Don't form a corporation, it's not necessary and limits what you can personally do. If you own it personally, load up on insurance- people today are very litigious.

Name your buildings if you wish but nothing too majestic, people tend to sue companies with big corporate sounding names. Why put a target on your back? For this same reason, it's actually good to be mortgaged, having a nice fat, paid-for property to sue makes lawyers salivate.

ALWAYS hire real, regular contractors to do electrical work (especially), to prevent you from being sued if someone gets hurt. Don't be a do-it-yourselfer.

You may find it frustrating trying to use a Realtor to buy- they always want to get the maximum full market price and you're looking for a bargain if possible. Buy the first one that meets your criteria, if you hesitate and keep looking looking looking- good deals go fast.

You make your money in real estate largely when you ***buy*** the property. In other words, pay a price that gives you a decent rate of return. Don't count on being able to raise rents and for there to be appreciation in order to justify the investment.

If you form an LLC, one hard-and-fast rule is you must use the exact name of the LLC in everything you do connected with that property. Tenants, vendors- all **must know** that they are dealing with an LLC. Tenants rent checks and vendor bills must be made out to the LLC, not to you.

The reason to use an LLC is if sued, they are limited to the assets of that LLC, which protects your other assets. That's another reason why you should not do certain repairs yourself, if you do, now they can go after you personally.

You will have to deal with a commercial banker if an LLC and pay a higher mortgage rate. No way around that.

In the near future, I'll be writing a book devoted to this topic of real estate investment. I will show how to use QuickBooks to easily do all the bookkeeping easily. You will be able to just print reports after year-end and hand them to your tax prep person to do your Schedule E. I will show how to evaluate all the financial aspects before you buy.

Chapter 9

RETIREMENT

The concept of retirement is relatively new. The main reason the concept came about in the last 70 years or so is because of life expectancy. People used to work until they dropped dead or could not physically do it anymore.

And people just didn't live this long before. The Mickey Mantle saying, *"If I had known I was going to live this long, I would have taken better care of myself."* always makes me laugh.

Newer still is the notion of retirementat 65 is changing again from quitting your job at 65 and taking up pure leisure like golf, knitting, building birdhouses to being more active and productive. Financial recession crises that wiped out peoples' savings didn't help either. And if you are lucky enough to love what you do, why retire at all?

My best advise is that it's best to have **options**. If you want to quit, then quit. If you want to keep working, then do that. If you want to dial it back and just work part-time, do that. The point is to give yourself options to do whatever you want. <u>Options</u> should be the goal. Options = freedom.

Retirement should be thought of as providing for your old age… so that you have options when the time comes, if you want to stop working you can, you're not forced to work to earn a living.

Social Security is an extremely poor investment component of your retirement. Your own invested retirement funds will grow much, much better in the free market. Your social security that you paid into all your working life can't even be passed on to your heirs. Social Security was only originally intended as a minimum safety net so people were spared being destitute. It used to be a trust fund, set aside, now the government has spent it all. It now covers millions who never worked, are disabled, and pays those who won't work by claiming a disability. When Social Security was originally enacted for 65 year olds, life expectancy was about 61.7.

I always disliked advise on calculating what you need saved/invested to retire. What is the point of that? I know it's supposed to motivate you, but it usually is just depressing and discourages you. I suggest not bothering. Anything that depresses your attitude should be avoided. You know what? It is what it is. You set aside as much as you are able while living the lifestyle for yourself and your family, and when you retire from active work, if you do, then you'll have what you have. There's no point stressing out over it for 40 years. Do your best and live life happy, not feeling guilty and inadequate. ***Remember the 15% rule, then you don't need to worry about any of this!***
I don't think you should live poor so you can die rich. Don't leave your kids a bunch of money- it will only turn them lazy and with a sense of entitlement for your money. We've all seen spoiled little rich kids, you're not doing them any favors.

Your goal in working toward retirement options is to give yourself the option, as best you can, of not being dependent on linear income from a job, where you trade hours (and freedom) for dollars. You want to end up with the option to live on only passive income if that's what you want (or if you can't work) at that time. Passive income are investments such as rental, dividend, interest, capital gain, profits.

I don't believe in postponing happiness until some future
retirement time and only then will you be living the lifestyle you
want. Live your life *now* while setting aside something for the
future.

People often orient themselves to primarily focus on the past, or
sometimes the future. In my case, I used to be too future-oriented.
I'll be happy later when... It's like focusing on the horizon, which
is artificial, and you can never actually reach it. Just as the horizon
is a visible point only from your current perspective, the future is a
mental construct and doesn't actually exist.

Some live in the past. The best parts of their lives all reside in the
past. It's pointless to think so much about the past, not only are
you giving up on anything in the present and future ever being as
good as the past, but the past is gone, there is nothing you can do
about it now to change it.

The only thing that is truly real is of course, the present. Today.
Plan for the future, yes, of course. Remember the past from time-
to-time, sure. But today is the only real thing you have to work
with. Learn to live in the present, be happy in the present. Do
things today that your future self will remember and thank you for.

Chapter 10

STARTING A BUSINESS

Many dream… few actually do. Only about 6-8% of the population is self-employed. Most people only wish from time to time they started a business. Small business is the driving force behind new job creation- most new jobs come from small business, not big companies.

We Americans largely established the idea that wealth could be *created* through capitalism. In other systems, people are kept poor and dependent by theft of their work by people in power who create nothing. That's why, in less than 250 years, we flew past countries with thousands of years history in economic progress of our people.

From a very young age, I knew I wanted to run my own business. I had no clue doing what, I just knew I wanted to be an independent business owner. I took me a long time because I had a family I needed to support, but I did it finally and have never been happier. I was miserable all the time when I had to work for someone else, started very small and very part-time and built it up slowly (bootstrapping) until it was big enough to give up my "day job".

It is crucial to be able to plan finances if you ever hope to start, and keep, a business. If you can't manage your personal finances, the major subject of this book, then you can't hope to ever run a business successfully.

I want you to think of successfully running a business as largely managing the cash that flows through it, so that you end up with a profit. Businesses fail when they run out of cash, even though there can be many reasons for it, it's the cash flow that counts. *Cash is king* is a true saying.

The owner's job is to oversee the cash in and out, while providing whatever it is your business does for its customers. Can you tell I'm an Accountant? *In a world of hammers, everything looks like a nail*. I know. But all the wonderful ideas in the world won't grow and last if you're not minding the cash flow. If you're not pricing enough or controlling your costs, there won't be any profit left to pay you for all your hard work.

What is your business idea?

Don't start a business because you have something you want to sell or do… nobody cares. Start a business because you are going to fulfill a desire or fix a pain actual customers need done. See the difference? People will buy from you for THEIR reasons… not for your reasons.

It's not what you sell- it's what, what you sell, does for them. In marketing your business, always emphasize the **benefits**, not the **features**. Don't, as most do, simply list ALL the things your business does… boring and nobody cares! Explain to them the **results** they get- **ultimately that's all they care about**!

Narrow your scope. **Not "everyone" is your customer**. Write down who your ideal customer is in detail, what is their worldview? Where do they hang out, what do they read, what other things do they believe in? **What is their pain?** What prevents them from acting, from buying right now? Build a demographic profile on paper.

Resist the temptation to copy your competitors in offering exactly everything they do so you'll fit in. Be sure to give potential customers a reason to choose you that ***they*** care about. Your goal is to make doing business with you the *path of least resistance*. No grief.

I encourage you to take the time to think deeply about these things and to write it all down, *before you start anything*. It will help you have a sense of purpose, and keep you moving in the right direction.

Tasks you will need to do to actually start your business: (In This Order)
- Line up a lawyer, CPA, banker, and insurance agent.
- Decide what type of entity the company should be. (use a business lawyer- and the lawyer typically will get you the EIN)
- Choose a name.
- File for a fictitious name in your state if needed.
- Obtain an E.I.N.
- Obtain a business license if needed in your area.
- Register the domain name.
- Open a business checking account.
- Arrange insurance coverages needed.

Ideally, a great business name contains what you do or *sounds like* what you do. It always bewilders me when I see a vehicle with signage that says something like, Apex Enterprises, D.P. # 34678934. What does that mean? Why bother advertising? I have no clue what they do. What's the point? A tagline to your company name should state the primary benefit THE CUSTOMER gets.

Use QuickBooks desktop to run your company. It's the most popular with approximately 80% of the market for good reason, it's powerful yet very intuitive to use. Keep business and personal finances completely separate.

Many successful people who got wealthy did it by owning a business. It's one of the best ways to build a better life for you and your family. It's all about living in a state of *freedom*.
My next book is going to be exclusively for small business owners… coming soon!

Appendix A

USING SOFTWARE

I recommend using QuickBooks Desktop if you want to computerize your personal finances. It works just as well for personal as it does for a business. Use it to enter and pay bills, to record income and transfers to savings accounts, and for reconciling those accounts to the bank statements.

I do not recommend Quicken or QuickBooks Online; they are not as simple and straightforward to use and Online is much more expensive in the long run. The desktop version is much more customizable and has much better reports.

Use Microsoft Excel for tasks where you need to do routine calculations. Construct the spreadsheet by separating inputs from outputs. Have an area where only inputs are entered in one place, and the spreadsheet is built to use the inputs with formulas to calculate and present the results. One of the main reasons to use a spreadsheet is so you avoid hand-calculating which can lead to errors, also saving a lot of time.

Another useful technique in Excel is to freeze panes so as you scroll right or down, the header information stays in view. Here's another quick tip: to automatically resize columns easily, left click and drag across all the columns to resize. (columns will be highlighted.) Then let go, and double-click between any two columns. Presto! The easiest way to build simple arithmetic formulas is the Pointing method. Starting in the cell where the result will show, start with the = sign, then click (point) to other cells, using the + - * / keys, even on different tabs, and when done hit Enter.

You can have Excel for your dynamic budget and Reserves spreadsheets and use QuickBooks to track all your finances, and produce reports to update the budget with your actual numbers each month. And if you reconcile the bank statement every month, you'll always be accurate and on top of your money.

I like having an online Ally savings account. When I transfer my 15% at the time I make any deposits, it only takes a minute.

Appendix B

RESOURCES

Intuit QuickBooks   (Desktop version, not Online or Quicken)

Microsoft Excel   (Desktop version, not Office 365)

LegalZoom (or a local business attorney preferably)

Ally Bank (setup with your checking account- then do "transfers" rather than deposits)

Firefox web browser (my preferred, although some banks don't play well with it.)

Keirsey Temperament Sorter II- a test to determine personality type

DISC- The Innermetrix DISC Index- test for behavioral tendencies.
https://www.16personalities.com
16 Personalities- Personality test-

StrengthFinder- book and testing

Other works by Bruce Van Cleve found at
www.rockledgerinc.com

Appendix C

RECOMMENDED READING AND WATCHING

Fox Business Channel

The Kiplinger Letter (newsletter)

Dan Sullivan books (StrategicCoach.com)

John T. Reed books (JohnTReed.com)

Glossary

***1031 Like-Kind Exchange*-** exchanging your fully depreciated property for another similar property to avoid selling and triggering capital gain taxes.

401(k) A (pre-tax) retirement investment vehicle that is Federal Income tax free (not Soc. Sec. or Med, State, local), usually as a deduction from pay and often a percentage is matched by the employer. (the match is an instant rate-of-return, free money)

Capitalism A system of economics where wealth is created by increasing cooperation among strangers, and where capital flows freely to where it is best utilized without any government intervention.

***Churn*-** excessive buying and selling by a broker to generate commissions.

Discretionary Not necessary for life, a want or desire, but not a true need.

Dynamic budget Estimated numbers that get replaced with actual, real numbers as each month is over, and future numbers revised if needed. The best way to have predictability.

E.I.N. Employer Identification Number. A number assigned to a business entity by the I.R.S.

Essential Necessary to stay alive.

Emergency Fund completely liquid cash cushion kept at all times in the checking account for unforeseen bills that suddenly happen. Beyond this amount, savings (accessible in days) enough to cover several month's worth of bills.

FDIC- Federal Deposit Insurance Corporation. $250,000 of deposits per depositor, per bank is insured against bank default.

Fictitious Name also known as a d.b.a. (doing business as). An unincorporated name you use to name your business including or beyond your name and what you do. Registered with the state.

Investing Long term money which is not touched for any spending, allowed to grow over time.

REIT- Real Estate Investment Trust. Kind of like a mutual fund for income properties.

Reserves Money saved toward future needs. The opposite of credit spending.

Roth IRA Amounts invested are after tax (you've already paid taxes), grow tax free and are withdrawn tax free when you're older. Roth's are best if you anticipate your income being more over time and in retirement.

Sinking Fund- setting aside money to replace an asset sometime in the future.

Solvency Income and assets are equal to or exceed expenditures. Ability to meet all your obligations without resorting to borrowing money.

Bibliography

Controlling Your Personal Finances David F. Owens 1937

The Simple Life Charles Wagner 1901

Modern Business Personal Finances C. Elliott Smith 1957

How To Get Started In Real Estate Investments John T. Reed 2006

Unique Ability Dan Sullivan 2009

The Power of Now Eckhart Tolle 1999

Profit First Mike Michalowicz 2014

The Millionaire Mind Thomas J. Stanley, Ph.D. 2000